Show Well, Sell Well

*103 Simple, Low-Cost Things to do
That Will Help Your Property
Show and Sell its Best*

by

Dawn Romance

iUniverse books may be ordered through booksellers or by contacting:

iUniverse
1663 Liberty Drive
Bloomington, IN 47403
www.iuniverse.com
844-349-9409

ISBN: 978-1-4401-7739-2 (sc)
ISBN: 978-1-4401-7738-5 (e)

Print information available on the last page.

iUniverse rev. date: 08/31/2021

In real estate....

Either move down the field or off of it;
just don't stay in the same position.

Contents

Preface

I have seen many homes over the years that would have sold faster and for a better price if only the seller had addressed some of the basic items that are important when showing a home. This book is written for anyone who wants to sell their home and is not sure what the best things are to do to get it ready. Think of it as a guideline to get you started. To get the most out of this book, it's important for you to be honest enough with yourself if a situation applies to you. And if an issue comes up that is not on my list, don't let that stop you from dealing with it either.

The best advice I can give you... To get the most out of your home sale, be open to what is being said to you and have a willingness to take action.

Chapter 1
Look, Ready, Action

For over 20 years I have seen all types of homes, everything from those about to be torn down to those that were truly beautiful. As a real estate agent in the Central Florida market, there is great opportunity to see it all. But regardless of what type of home you have, it is how you show your home that counts when selling it. Moreover, I believe that most homes can be wonderful in their own right. They may not have the latest infinity pool or granite countertops, but that doesn't mean they can't stand out. I wrote this book to illustrate very basic and inexpensive things you can do to improve the look of your property and make it the great one to remember when it is on the market.

The biggest thing to do when getting ready to sell your home is to look—*really* look—at your entire property, inside and out. Not as the resident who has lived there for the last seven years, or however long you have lived there, but look from the eyes of someone who would want to buy it. This requires a different set of eyes—a fresh set of eyes.

If you cannot do it for yourself, find someone who will be honest enough to tell you the truth. If no friends or family step up to the plate, calling a local real estate agent can be the next best thing. You may not like what you hear, but I promise you that all of it is said from the perspective of getting you the most money for your property. Most real estate agents work on commission—the more you make, the more they make.

This leads me to my next point. If you are going to put your property on the market, be ready to do so, *really ready*. This means cleaning up the woodworking, landscaping, and any other *I haven't had time to*

3

finish projects. Don't wait for a prospective buyer to tell you that they didn't even look in the backyard because they couldn't maneuver safely back there. This wastes everyone's time: yours, the buyer's, and the real estate agent's.

WARNING! Selling your home requires effort on your part. Either do the work yourself or hire the appropriate person to do so. It is in everyone's best interest to get someone who knows how to do the work. So many people think that in doing it themselves they will always save money. That's not the case if you don't know what you are doing, especially if you are not handy. Use your real estate agent as a litmus test as to whether or not you should take on the project or hire someone. Many real estate agents know good handymen for small jobs. The right or wrong person doing the project reflects proportionally on how the house shows as well as how it will inspect and thus, sells.

All of this being said, I am going to leave you to my list. I have noted items that are good to do daily, weekly, and monthly. I have also highlighted a few of the deep clean items. But please know that all of it is important!

Daily— **D**

Weekly— **W**

Monthly— **M**

Deep Clean— **DC**

Chapter 2
Say Yes to Your Yard

1. **Keep it short**. Even if you have weeds, keep your yard mowed. They will be less noticeable. What's more, buyers think that if you are not doing something as simple as mowing, then the rest of the property is going to be bad. **W**

2. **Think green**. This is the color your lawn should be. If not, check your sprinkler system. If you don't have one, get a hose and sprinkler and start moving it around the property regularly. The best time to water is either early

morning or at night. And if your lawn has bugs, get a lawn pest service before the entire yard is gone!

3. **Do your hedges have edges?** When was the last time someone trimmed them? Are some dead? Dead bushes distract from healthy-looking ones. Uneven bushes make your yard look out of control. **W**

4. **Give it definition**. A mowed yard is nice, but a mowed and *edged* yard is noticeably better. **W**

5. **Do the vines have it?** Have you let your landscaping get to the point that your shrubs are getting strangled by vines? Save them! Have you let vines creep onto your house? Get them off! Your plants need to live, and your house doesn't need a roadway for insects to get inside. Plus, it is taking off the paint. **DC**

6. **Mulch!** It is the best and cheapest fix for making your yard pop. At $5 a bag, start buying. It is great for children's play areas, flower beds, and bushes.

7. **Pick one and go healthy**. Plants should be living or gone. No one wants to buy a "new" house with dead azaleas. **DC**

8. **Moderation**. It is the best word for outdoor decorations.

9. **Add color.** Easy! Add some flowering plants around the entrance and patio areas. Even if it is just a small area, it will create a pleasant draw to your property.

10. **To love them is to cut them.** Trees that is. If you are in an area with heavy tree canopy, this is for you. It can concern a buyer to see huge branches looming over the house, the garage, or the guest house. It is a good idea to have a licensed tree service inspect your trees periodically. And if trimming is needed, take care of it – for the sake of the tree as well as your property.

11. **They're built for privacy!** Walk along your fence line. Is your fence still doing its job? Are there boards in need of a tack down? Are there missing boards? Are there holes under your fence? The answers are all around your property. **DC**

Chapter 3
Exceptional Exteriors and Entrances

12. **First impressions are lasting impressions.** Stand at your front door. Do you have a doorbell? Does it work? Does your door handle work? Does your front door need to be painted or replaced? And if it has glass, when was the last time you cleaned it? Would you want to come in the house just from standing at the front door? **DC**

13. **Your entrance, part two.** Okay, you are still standing at your front door. Now look up. Is the entryway full of little cobwebs and tree debris? At the very least, get a broom and wipe it all off. This one costs nothing and does wonders to keep buyers from being grossed out at your front door. **DC**

> *I showed a house once where the agent went on and on about how well the seller maintained the house, especially the floors. However, when my buyers and I got to the front door, it was obvious that the seller never looked up. The entire front porch ceiling, door trim, and window frames were coated in brown cobwebs and tree debris. We weren't even in the door yet, and I could tell by the look on my buyers' faces that this home was going to be a no for them.*

14. **Your entrance, part three.** Look around. What is on or around your front porch or entrance? Your child's skateboard? A phonebook still in the plastic bag it came

in four weeks ago? Put it all away. Your entrance should be clean *and* clutter free. **DC**

15. **Make it nice.** Have a nice entrance mat. Don't go for cute or funny. Save that for the side door. Make it size appropriate too. Too small looks cheap. It should be close to the width of your door.

16. **Do a lap.** Just around your house; that's all! Is the left shutter still hanging at an angle? What have you stockpiled on the side of the house because you couldn't deal with it? Is there any painting or caulking needed? The answers matter to the buyer, and they should to you too! **DC**

17. **Do a second lap.** This time look up at the eaves—the underneath part of your roof line that extends beyond your house. Most newer homes have metal eaves. For visual purposes and to prevent critters from getting in, make sure there are no missing pieces. Older homes typically have wooden eaves. These require more maintenance. For both, make sure you don't have any bug nests or other debris. And get the wood repaired if you have wood rot.**DC**

18. **One more lap.** This time you want to look at your light fixtures. Are there any missing bulbs, rusting fixtures, broken or missing glass? When a buyer walks around your home, they are noting it all! **DC**

19. **Got gutters?** This one requires that you stand at least a few feet, if not at the end of your curb, from your home. If you have white gutters, they should look white. Not green. Not black. A bucket of soap and water, and maybe some bleach, should take care of it. Also, gutters should not be full or have anything growing in them. It defeats the main purpose of moving water away from your house! **DC**

20. **The Big Top.** No, I am not referencing a tent, but rather your roof. If you have a shingle roof with some fungus, get it cleaned before any showings. The safest bet is to have a professional do it. If done incorrectly, you could be taking granules off your shingles before their time. If repairs are needed, make sure they are done by a licensed roofer. Reputable ones stand by a warranty, and it's usually transferable to a buyer.

21. **Built before 1970?** If so, there is a chance your home is built on a crawl space. This means your home was built up and there is a space between the ground and your flooring. Homes that have crawl spaces have vents around the house and a larger one to get underneath. Make sure landscaping has not piled up around the vents. Keep the larger access doors cleared from shrubbery too. Crawl spaces need to breathe so they can dry out if water gets in them.

Chapter 4
Windows, Doors, and More

22. **The only film that everyone considers bad.** It's the one on your windows. This is an inside and outside job! For the second story windows, there is an outside cleaner that attaches to your garden hose. Better yet, hire a professional window cleaner! **DC**

23. **It shouldn't take your whole body to move them.** We're talking about sliding glass doors here. At the very least, spray the rollers with some WD-40; at most, replace them.

24. **No sunroom is complete without them!** Think of any home and garden magazine you've ever looked at with a sunroom. They *always* have beautiful French doors in the picture. You may not have the sunroom, but if you have French doors, make sure they look and work well. Clean glass?—check. Handle works?—check. Lock works?—check. Door rot free?—check.

25. **They keep the critters out and the view in.** Whether it is pool screens or window screens, none of them should be green, torn, or missing. **DC**

I have shown my share of homes where the seller has left the screens torn or missing because that is how their pet comes and goes. The question on the buyer's mind is, "What else comes and goes?"

---

26. **Will open on command.** Unless they are broken, I am referring to your garage doors. Are they beaten up or dented? Are the windows broken? If so, get them fixed.

27. **Open for the world to see?** If you happen to have a carport, clear it out if possible. Otherwise, keep the items to a minimum. Having too many things can overwhelm some buyers. **DC**

Chapter 5

Accessories that Accent

28. **Keep them looking the way they were designed.** Play forts, trampolines, basketball hoops, and other outside play things should be set up as they were intended to be. If not, fix them or take them down.

> *I have seen play sets that are barely standing upright, torn trampolines, basketball hoops weighted down by concrete blocks, and disassembled play forts strewn about yards. The buyer's first question is, "Are the sellers taking that with them?" The second question is, "How do I get rid of it?"*

29. **Hoses should be hidden.** Enough said.

30. **What do a plastic fish, a crooked post, and a rusted door have in common?** They are all things that your mailbox should not be.

31. **So how does the shed look**? If the answer is bad, take it down.

32. **Have pots, need plants.** So you bought some beautiful pots in hopes of planting some new plants, but that is as far as you got. Either remove them or get some plants.

33. **Would you sit on it**? Do *you* or the critters around your property use your yard furniture? If someone couldn't pay you to sit down on it, then it's not acceptable for a buyer to see it in that condition. If the cushions are too

far gone, remove them. It's great if you can replace them with newer ones, but better gone than dirty. **DC**

34. **Wood, charcoal, or gas.** It doesn't matter what type of grill you have, just clean it up afterward. At the very least, put the cover back on. And don't forget the tongs.

Chapter 6

Clean and Clear

35. **Tripping hazard ahead.** Pool equipment and toys can be unsightly and dangerous if left strewn about. Make sure toys are put away. Equipment should be in the pool doing its job or put away as well.

36. **Clean your concrete.** Pressure washers remove dirt like no other method. Clean off your driveway, walkways, patio, and deck areas. This is a great way to make your

property really stand out! Go the cheaper route and rent one at your local hardware store. **DC**

37. **Cracked up?** Check walkways and driveways for raised and cracked surfaces. Minor ones are typically not a big deal. But if one person has tripped over it, know that there will be another.

38. **They should be inviting**. When you see your pool, you should want to take a dip, or at least think it is a nice idea. Keep up with maintenance and chemicals. **W**

39. **Disappear debris!** Removing miscellaneous debris from around your property gives it a much better appearance. An air blower does the trick every time. **W**

This is one of my favorite items on the list. And since I lack the skill, I hire someone to do it for me.

40. **People will peek.** If you have a stand alone spa, this is for you! When you cover the spa, please make sure you are still maintaining it or you empty out the water. Otherwise, it is not a good scene.

41. **Cars, bikes, and scooters.** None of them should be in the driveway when your house is being shown. Good is having them in your garage or carport. For cars, better is having them gone.

Chapter 7
Order in the House

42. **People want to know what is in them.** It is commonplace for buyers to want to open up and see inside your cabinets and closets. Packed? Need some organizing? Spend the time! **DC**

43. **Go all the way!** Not to the laundry room. Not to the garage. When the trash bag is full, take your trash all the way out to your outside trash cans.

44. **Only one thing should be dirty in this room.** And that is your clothes in your laundry room. Baskets are a great way to keep it organized too.

45. **Do you have utter clutter?** Do you have to maneuver to get from one room to another? Rooms should have good pathways for people to walk through. Too much is distracting at best and overwhelming at worst. **Ⓓ**

46. **Let's keep antics to a minimum!** Refrigerators tend to be the bulletin boards in the kitchen. Less is good. Minimal is better. And nothing is best.

47. **No, it is not the real estate agent's job to pick up any of it!** Laundry should be in one of four places: the washer, the dryer, the dresser, or the hamper. **Ⓓ**

> *I have seen dirty laundry in every area of a home, from the foyer to family room to the stairs and anywhere else you can think of. And it's never been a pretty sight.*

48. **Bins, baskets, and boxes.** Any of these will work when putting your children's toys away for showings.

49. **99 items on the wall.** It's better to go less on walls. It's actually more! Couple of things worth consideration on this one - 1. Try to minimize collections, personal pictures and miscellaneous knick knacks. 2. Even one animal head doesn't go over well with some prospective buyers.

50. **And #49 goes for these too!** Just like your walls, your shelves should not be jam-packed.

Chapter 8

Clean to Be Seen

51. **This one is next to Godliness!** Cleanliness! Much of this book talks about cleaning the many parts of your home. Not sure if you can do it or want to take it on? Hire a cleaning service for regular visits or at least a one time deep clean. Then maintain that clean! If you want someone to imagine themselves in your home, make it as inviting as possible.

52. **Susan swipes sills on Saturday.** This one may be a tongue twister, but it's easy to wipe down windowsills that collect noticeable dust and other debris. **Ⓜ**

53. **Your bare feet will appreciate this one.** Floors should be clean if you are showing your home. Look for carpet stains. If they don't come out or the carpet has had a good life, it is better to replace it than to give a credit. Just go neutral on the replacement. **Ⓦ**

> *I showed a home once where there was actually dog poop on the carpet.* **Watch Your Step** *was the motto that day!*

54. **Fire!** No one wants to hear those words unless it's in a fireplace. And if the wood is not burning, then it should be cleaned out.

55. **Ah, natural light—wait, is that a roach?** Skylights offer great light in a room, but look up. Is it time to take the

cover off and clean it out? Are there old water stains from a leak you fixed a year ago? **DC**

56. **The only bunnies no one likes!** And those are the dust bunnies on your furniture. Polish please! **W**

57. **Should be seen and clean**. Countertops should be clean and have minimal items on them. People want to see how much space they offer. **D**

58. **Don't even think of stacking them up.** Sinks should be empty and clean. **D**

59. **"Splish splash," says the food to the backsplash**. The backsplash is the space between the countertop and the cabinet. Tile, drywall, and stone are okay to be there. Crusted food and crayon drawings are not.

60. **It should be the color it was intended to be.** Grout is the material that outlines and adheres tiles, such as your floor tiles, shower tiles, or tiled kitchen countertops. Keep the mold and dirt away. You may need to get a scrub brush for this one.

61. **This one can cost as little as $3**. A new shower liner does wonders for so little!

62. **If it is where you clean yourself, it should be clean too.** Buyers always look behind the shower curtain. So when it comes to tubs and showers, just say no to soap scum and mold. **W**

63. **Keep it shut.** It's the best way to show a toilet. Clean is a must as well! **W**

64. **Squeegee please**! This is a cheap fix to keep shower doors clean. **D**

65. **They can have skid marks too!** Look up at your air vents. Does it look like dirt is shooting out of them? At a minimum, wipe off the dirt, and at best, get your ducts cleaned. And make sure the vents are secured to the ceiling. **DC**

66. **Who is the cleanest of them all?** It is the mirror mirror on the wall, thanks to some window cleaner. Trimming out old mirrors can be a nice upgrade. **W**

Chapter 9

Big and Small— Take Care of It All

67. **Pick one again**. What is true for the outside is equally true for the inside on this one. Make sure your plants look healthy or remove them. **DC**

68. **Not everyone has a designer's eye.** Or a designer's budget to match. Pillows and throws are inexpensive ways to enhance old furniture. However, if you still have the glider rocker from when your six-year-old was a baby, it might be time to store it away until you are sure you are done with it.

69. **Size matters.** It's important for furniture to be in proportion to the room. Too much and the room seems small. Too little and the buyer struggles with the room

size. There is such a thing as just right. P.S. Most workout equipment takes up big space (hint, hint).

70. **The bathroom necessities.** Toilet paper and towels. Have toilet paper on the roll. Hang up your towels. But before you do that, look at your toilet paper and towel rack holders. Are they just one turn of a screw from falling off the wall? Secure them back. Clean towels nicely folded on the towel racks are a bonus for everyone.

71. **Newer goes a long way!** You don't need a high-end dishwasher for the buyer to appreciate a newer one. Updated appliances go a long way with prospective buyers.

72. **Moderation**. Again, it is the best word for decorations. This time think interior.

73. **Push 1 for away. Push 2 for never been used**. If you have an alarm system, make sure it is working, regardless of whether it is connected to a service or not. Or tell the prospective buyers it hasn't been used in the last ten years, and it conveys *as-is*.

74. **So what's that cover plate on the ceiling?** Oh right, it's where your smoke alarm used to be until you took it down because of the annoying beeping noise from the dying battery. Replace both!

75. **A bedroom favorite.** Ceiling fans. A layer of dust lining the edge of ceiling fans is not attractive. They should be included in the monthly clean category. **Ⓜ**

76. **The stuffed ones are for kids only.** Keep stuffed animals to your kids' bedrooms. They are not cute anywhere else.

77. **Every room has one.** Switches are used mainly for lights and ceiling fans. The plates shouldn't be cracked or broken. And they should work! **DC**

Chapter 10
Look All Around You

78. **Favorite color—real estate beige.** When painting, go neutral. If you like bright, vibrant colors, that is great. Just know they can overwhelm some buyers to think it would be difficult to paint over. Also, do you have wallpaper? Busy florals and other strong patterns tend to give buyers the same feeling.

79. **It finishes a room.** Crown molding is a great way to add a finishing touch to a room. Already have it? Then check to see if it needs to be caulked or touched up. Still stained dark from the 1980s? Paint and go lighter.

80. **The fingerprints have it!** Walk around the inside of your house and look at door trims and walls to see where the popular spots are. If a wipe-down works, great. If a touch up is needed, get the paint out. **DC**

81. **So how many times did Johnnie crash his toy car against them?** Baseboards should be a part of the deep clean when listing your home. Do they need to be touched up? Caulked? Painted? **DC**

82. **Their job is to get thrown down, walked on, shaken out, and then they are ready to do it all over again.** Just talking about rugs here. They should enhance a room. If they don't, they should be cleaned, replaced, or removed altogether. It doesn't matter if it is in your bathroom or dining room.

83. **They're not for storage.** Stairs should be free and clear of everything.

84. **You can get away with it here.** Garages don't have to be ideal. If this is the only place to store items, then box away. Better here than taking up space inside the house. But be realistic; your garage needs to be seen too. **DC**

85. **The space where few go.** Check what is up in your attic. Sometimes things up there are for your eyes only. Just know all of it must go!

I have seen homes with all sorts of things in the attic. One had a concrete parking bumper, one had an abandoned oil tank, and one had some very personal photos and DVDs. You just never know!

86. **Go below and know.** We don't have many basements in Florida, but if you have one and use it as a living area, treat it as you would your interior. If you just store items there, treat it like you would your garage.

Chapter 11
Make It Work for You

87. **Monster motor!** Does your bathroom exhaust fan sound loud enough to be confused with a 747 overhead? Then it's time to repair or replace it.

88. **You always have to go through this!** I am not talking about anything else other than doors. But if you have old doors, it's best to replace them with newer ones. Just know it could lead to new hinges and handles! Touch them up at the very least. There should not be any holes or scuffs. Handles should be completely attached. If they make noise, use a little WD-40.

89. **The 3 H's.** I am referring to the **H**ardware, which includes **H**andles and **H**inges on drawers and cabinets. Make sure they are there and working as they should. Hanging on doesn't count. **DC**

90. **Make it!** Do as your mother says and make your bed in the morning. Unmade beds are distracting. Clean sheets are a must too. **D**

> *Believe it or not, there is such a thing as a dirty sheet smell. Unfortunately, I have smelled this enough to know what it is!*

91. **Safe and secure.** Banisters, railings, and any other handles used to maneuver throughout your house should be secure. When someone new is walking up

your stairs and they go to grab the handrail, it shouldn't move with them. **DC**

92. **Have on hand**. Caulk is one of the simplest fixes. It works to seal up crown molding, drywall, faucets, and so much more!

93. **Make it a great turn on!** Faucets are a great item to upgrade. Everyone loves that handle that comes out of the spout. At the very least, stop any dripping or leaking.

94. **Breathe well, part one.** Your AC filter should be changed once a month. And they cost less than $10! **M**

95. **Breathe well, part two.** An AC system has two parts: the air handler (usually in a closet or your garage) and the compressor (always outside). Buyers want to know 1. how old it is, 2. when it was last serviced, and 3. how many you have. And for those of you that don't know, your AC system appreciates a yearly service.

Chapter 12

Amazing Atmosphere

96. **Open sesame!** Blinds should be open or up for showings. Most people like light. As for drapes, if you have an old house where they have been there for decades, remove them. There's no telling what's living in them! Otherwise, keep them as open and clean as possible.

97. **Whether it is Fahrenheit or Celsius.** Be aware of the temperature in your house. Too hot or cold makes people think you need a new AC or furnace. Plus, if people are uncomfortable, they are not going to stay. And you want them to!

98. **The nose knows!** Have a friend or relative walk through your home. How does it smell? Like dog? Like smoke? Like the fish you fried last night? You may need something as simple as a scented candle. Or you may need to take greater action.

99. **What is that I hear?** TV shows on—*no*. Movie theater entertainment systems on—*as appropriate*. Music on—*yes*. But go soothing. It should blend into the background. Nothing on? That can work too!

100. **Let there be light!** Replace burnt out light bulbs. Then make sure the lights are on. It's so simple and so important for any room. Extra kudos for getting the energy efficient ones! **DC**

101. **They are not always the same without you there.** Your pet may be the sweetest thing when you are around, but take *you* out of the picture and put *them* with a stranger. That is the case when you leave your pets roaming the house when a real estate agent and buyer come by to see it. Oh, let's add a four-year-old who desperately wants to pet it. Not good! That being said, this one doesn't always have an easy answer. It's best if your pet can be gone. Another option is for them to be properly crated for the showing. Take them for a walk or drive around the block. Or put them in the garage or basement, as appropriate. If that is not feasible, pick one of the guest bedrooms. Give this one good consideration for both your pet's sake and for how best to show your home.

102. **Family and friends.** The best case scenario is that they are not in the house when you have a showing. Other good options are to have them sit outside on the patio, go for a walk, or take a short drive. But once inside, neither they nor the buyers feel comfortable.

103. **The owner, the seller, and you**. Be gone—not in your office, not outside. Gone. Let the buyer imagine themselves there without you!

Chapter 13
Think of It as a To Do List

Here is a quick and easy look at what to address for showing your property.

Daily	Weekly
Clean countertops	Mow yard
Empty and clean sinks	Edge yard
Make your bed	Trim hedges
Pick up your laundry	Maintain the pool/spa
Wipe down shower doors	Air blow property clean
Declutter as possible	Clean floors
	Clean mirrors
	Clean toilets
	Clean shower/tub
	Polish furniture
	Vacuum carpet

Monthly	Deep Clean
Change air filter	Check plants, inside & out
Dust ceiling fans	Remove unwelcome vines
Dust blinds	Clean gutters
Clean windowsills	Inspect entire exterior
	Clean outside furniture
	Clean windows inside and out
	Pressure wash patios, walkways, & drive
	Clear out carport and garage, as possible
	Repair/replace screens as necessary
	Check your fencing
	Organize cabinets and closets
	Wipe down/touch up baseboards & walls
	Clean air vent dirt; ducts, if necessary
	Check skylights
	Check bulbs, switches, & hardware

Look to the back of this book for your *Have on Hand* 1 page tear-out list.

Chapter 14
Find, Fix, and Flexible

If all of this seems overwhelming, I promise you it's not. Here are a couple of things to keep in mind. First, look at where you live and the season you are in. This will play a factor for some of the items on my list, especially those referencing your yard. For example, in Florida there is a big difference between needing to mow your yard every week in August because it rains almost every day and only needing to mow it every couple of weeks in February since the grass is dormant then.

Secondly, if you don't know where to begin, just pick one thing to address. Your one thing may be to make sure there are no dishes in the sink. Great! Start there. Once you are good with doing that, go to the next item that you can manage to do and that you will do. Most of the things on my list don't need to be done in the exact timetable I gave, but it is offered as a guideline to keep up with regular maintenance. So if it's only five things on the list that get done this month, then that is five more things that will move you in the right direction when selling your home. Just remember— the more you do and, for most of the items, the more often you do it, the better your home will show and the better it will sell.

And speaking of remembering, keep reminding yourself that you are selling your home. This is worth repeating—you are *selling your home*. It is so important to be open to the buyer's comments. The market will tell you what it's willing to accept and what it's not. So if the dark drapes in the living room make people feel like they are walking into a cave, it doesn't matter what they cost or who passed them down to you, you need to fix the problem. You have many options as to what to do with them: put them up in the home you are moving to, store them away, sell them, or donate them. But the biggest thing is to fix the issue at hand, whatever it may be. Or you can price your home to reflect its current condition. So if the problem is an outdated kitchen, rather then spending thousands of dollars updating it, reduce your price to show buyers that you have taken that into consideration.

Third, do the best that you can. If you don't have the money to trim out old mirrors or anything else and all you can do is pick up, organize, and clean up, then do that. People appreciate a truly clean and picked up home. It shows you care and that you made an effort.

That being said, people understand that you are *living* in your home. Pleasing does not require perfection. Don't drive everyone crazy going overboard on being a clean freak. Let your children sit in the family room with a snack. Use your kitchen to eat your meals. Just be realistic with yourself on the time you need for clean up.

Lastly, be realistic with pricing your home. So often I hear people say that they *need* to get $25,000 or $50,000 (or whatever amount they have in their head) from their home after expenses. Let me say this as kindly as I can: the market doesn't think about what you need or what your feelings are or whether you have spent the last twenty years in your home. The market only cares about what is happening to similar properties like yours in the current market. It doesn't look back to what has been, and it doesn't look forward to what might be. Here are some factors that are at play and are worth serious consideration when pricing your home:

- ✓ The type of market you're in (seller versus buyer)
- ✓ How many homes like yours are on the market
- ✓ The sale price of similar homes that have sold in the last six months; extreme markets look at the last three months
- ✓ The current economic conditions

And as I conclude this book, let me say to all the sellers out there: I wish you the very best. Selling your home is personal, emotional, and exhausting! So take one day at a time and keep moving toward the next showing. And when you want to say "No" or "Not now" or

"I like it the way I have it" when feedback is presented to you from a prospective buyer, know you could be choosing your way over the possibility of making more money or a faster sale. It's all about choices – ask any real estate agent!

Have on Hand To Do List

Here is a quick and easy look at what to address for showing your property.

Daily

- ☐ Clean countertops
- ☐ Empty and clean sinks
- ☐ Make your bed
- ☐ Pick up your laundry
- ☐ Wipe down shower doors
- ☐ Declutter as possible

Weekly

- ☐ Mow yard
- ☐ Edge yard
- ☐ Trim hedges
- ☐ Maintain the pool/spa
- ☐ Air blow property clean
- ☐ Clean floors
- ☐ Clean mirrors
- ☐ Clean toilets
- ☐ Clean shower/tub
- ☐ Polish furniture
- ☐ Vacuum carpet

Monthly

- ☐ Change air filter
- ☐ Dust ceiling fans
- ☐ Dust blinds
- ☐ Clean window sills

Deep Clean

- ☐ Check plants, inside & out
- ☐ Remove unwelcome vines
- ☐ Clean gutters
- ☐ Inspect entire exterior
- ☐ Clean outside furniture
- ☐ Clean windows inside & out
- ☐ Pressure wash patios, walkways, & drive
- ☐ Clear out carport & garage, as possible
- ☐ Repair/replace screens as necessary
- ☐ Check your fencing
- ☐ Organize cabinets & closets
- ☐ Wipe down/touch up baseboards & walls
- ☐ Clean air vent dirt, ducts, if necessary
- ☐ Check skylights
- ☐ Check bulbs, switches & hardware

NOTES:

Add specific things about your property to address.

_____

_____

_____

_____

_____

_____

_____

_____

_____

_____

_____

_____

_____

_____

NOTES:

Add specific things about your property to address.

_____

_____

_____

_____

_____

_____

_____

_____

_____

_____

_____

_____

_____

_____

_____

_____

Printed in the United States
by Baker & Taylor Publisher Services